TIMELESS THOUGHTS

SHASHIKALA GADEPALLY

To all the poets who have inspired me

Contents

Contents

1. TIME

If time could be caged and locked!
If the clicking of the clock could be reversed,
If its fluttering wings could be clipped,
Time would go back in TIME.
What a wonder!
But knowing this eternal truth
THAT
Time and tide wait for none
we still yearn for the impossible ....
to put back the clock.
If time could fly into unknown realms
TIME TRAVEL WOULD NO MORE BE FICTIONAL
no more a fantasy.
How incredible-
tumbling into the past times
flinging into the future!
H.G. Wells' THE TIME MACHINE
would no more be a make-believe world.
A wow to the mind, so innovative, so creative
for thoughts that
drive away the monotony
usher in freshness and novelty
into Eliot's dreary 'Waste Land'.
Tossing and jostling

yet meticulous and brisk
TIME, in a jiffy, can alter lives.
Let not the mind wander into the bizarre past
or meander into the web of the future.
Let the present be the cherished legacy
let the present nourish the quest for eternity.

2. AT THE APPOINTED TIME

The buds blossom when it is time to bloom

The clouds gather when it is time to rain

The trees wear new leaves when time heralds Spring

The sea rushes inland when it is time to kiss the sand

And the waves rise and fall when it is time to tease the moon

Neither time nor the natural phenomena

happen in isolation

The bond that unifies them is a cosmic marvel

Does The Fall happen in Summer, or do the rains lash in Winter?

Time is the paragon of occurrences, natural or celestial.

Does the monsoon see the dazzling sunshine?

Time is the order of things in this universe

The coherence, if tampered with, shall hurl

our existence into a void

The interminable tumult and chaos

shall cripple the cosmic order

Let time be the guide

And our intellect, the chariot

together, we shall navigate the seas of the world

Let Time lead the journey

lest the cosmos turns topsy-turvy.

3. THE CHASE

The three hands seem to chase one another jovially
As though challenging themselves to prove their mettle
the hands move rhythmically, tirelessly
at the same pace, with precision
uncomplainingly towards their destination.
One move ahead second by second
The other keeps its tempo unhurriedly
And the small one is at ease
'I shall take my own sweet time to move.'
It seems to say, rejoicing its leisurely strides.
The small hand wonders at the second's hand
'What maketh thou run so swiftly?
Have a tryst with destiny?'
The minute's hand holds onto its tempo,
proving its consistent pursuit of the five-minute lap.
'The twine shall meet at the appointed hour.'
God proclaimed
And the minutes and the hour hand entwine
as the clock strikes the hour 12.
Time - a marvel
chases dreams, challenges worth
changes relationships transform minds
But its momentum is irreversible
Never drifting from its path

Consistently, constantly, it moves along its predestined trajectory.

• 5 •

4. DREAMS

Dreams come true.
Strive tirelessly
incessantly to build dreams
and pursue them with courage.
Chase your dreams
no dream is unattainable.
When the waking hours brim with passion,
new avenues unfold.
Nest those unconquerable dreams
that keep you awake
grab those moments
and dive into the unfathomable seas
spread your wings and soar high.
Let the waking moments strengthen your resolve
Ambitious dreams
challenge your grit
question your tenacity
doubt your pertinence.
Let your resolve be thy beacon light
in pursuit of dreams
that define your indomitable spirit.

5. DREAMS- A DIGRESSION?

"I slept and dreamt life is beauty
I woke and found life is duty."
(Louisa May Alcott)
Are dreams a lie
that disconnects one from reality?
Are dreams a digression from the path of duty?
A dream that
plunges one into self-doubt
questions the veracity of facts
rests on falsity
misrepresents ambition,
is truly an irretraceable departure.
Aren't dreams a wonderful dichotomy?
Unambitious sleepy dreams
wandering in a maze,
vibrant dreams
driven with passion in waking hours.
Colliding, entangling dreams find their way
through the mesh of life
one weaning away from reality
the other waking up to life.

6. MEMORIES

Memories - a treasure trove to cherish
nurture them with fondness
lest they melt away into oblivion
as the time fleets.
Gather those invaluable moments
that may not have meant much
but as time passes, the loss of a dear one
or the disconnect with a pal
may spur the cosy memories
of a beautiful evening spent together
Or a sunset on a seashore.
Let not the sands of time snatch away
moments of togetherness,
make long-lasting memories
That soothes your soul and cheers your spirit.
Aren't those memories
that connect you with the people of yore
a click there and a note here
a dried flower in the book
a scarf with initials
let not this album of joy fade
feed it with emotions
hold on with love.
Moments become memories

memories feed on experiences
experiences thrive on past moments.
Endless memories perpetuated
in the recesses of the mind
pop out reminiscing the precious feelings
the joy of the past moments.
String those bits to embellish the gone days
emotions and relationships.

7. THE ROAD

The muddy, slushy track
unpaved, worn out, wanting care,
awaits its turn cheerfully.
Complaining? Never
Compromising? always
never has it wailed about its poor state.
Acceptance is its forte, perseverance its nature
'The road not taken' by many
waits for someone
who shall change the course of its life
someone who shall willingly
tread on it to reach his destination.
The road then shall rejoice in its fulfilment.
Murky or filthy, bumpy or rugged
matters not
what matters-
it paves the way
for a journey through the thick and thin of life.

8. THE STREET

On either side of the street, an array of houses
the compound wall fails to separate the houses,
twin houses, they appear to be
no gap, no space
privacy a far-flung concept
It matters neither to the street
Nor to the housemates.
When is it that the inmates did not hear
the grumbling of the neighbours?
OR
The angry outbursts of the male inmates?
The aroma of the sweet dish
OR
the tangy smell of the roasted spices?
Not so easy to guess the house that grills the chicken
or cooks the fish.
it seems to permeate the air.
Infiltrating from one house to another surreptitiously
Making one neighbour wrinkle her nose
the other to relish.
The fragrance of the jasmine flowers
adorning the idols in the pooja room
the aroma of the incense sticks
filters into the neighbourhood.

The garbage tossed from this gate
scatters across the street,
nullifying the sweet scent of flowers.
Often, the home-makers are seen
spending hours at the gate talking across the street
from casual talk to serious themes
sometimes politics, often movies
more often, the gossip about so and so....
The joy of life seems to come alive
the street being their identity

9. THE LAMP POST

Illuminating the alleys
dispelling the darkness
enveloping the surroundings,
the lamp post stands upright
sharing its pride with the fellow lamps
posted as sentinels
driving away the fear of darkness
as people amble along the streets.
It smiles, remembering its origins
rooted in the ancient times
from clay lamp to metal
lamps graduating from era to era.
The oil lit to candle-fixed lamps
the lamp-posts share a history of antiquity to modernity.
The dusk saw the lighting of lamps
across the street, one after the other
AND
the lanes and by-lanes envying the streets
what more could a street as for?
Dim, yes, but it did brighten the dingy streets.
From sheer embellishments in the Victorian era
to purposeful illumination of the streets
as the phases changed from one to another
lamps have evolved to establish their merit.

Reflecting the culture and artistry of the bygone eras
to delineate the evolution of the mind
lamp-posts are no mere ornaments
they articulate the intellect at work.

10. SOLITUDE

Forlorn, away from the 'madding crowd'
I seek solace in the green woods
The long blades of grass, the carpet so green
the trickling water through the creeks
promise to hold me in a tight embrace
hold me close to their heart
where I feel the pulse throbbing with life.
My solitude, self-inflicted pain
to alleviate the hurt and the wounds
of unresolved relationships.
Yearning for tranquillity
seeking serenity in the lap of nature
The anguish of biting loneliness
amidst kith and kin is chaos immeasurable.
To unravel the mysteries of unspoken thoughts
to read the unsaid words
to feel the unexpressed emotions
solitude- a panacea.
Let the quietude seep into the turbulent mind
Let equanimity soak the soul
Let solitude be the strength I seek.
And then
as I rise and plough through relationships
my solitude shall accompany me through the maze.

11. THE WRITER IN ME

One day, I got up
with a strange feeling.
Maybe I thought
the disturbing dreams
played havoc with me.
As the day passed, the
feeling got stronger and better of me.
Neither shake off I could nor relate,
but that weird feeling persisted.
I took a stroll along the green track of my villa
And sipped hot coffee twice.
Feeling refreshed, I stood on the balcony
watching the waves lash against the shore
Just as my thoughts gripped my troubled mind, yet again.
Thoughts assailed me, feelings crushed me
my mind in a mayhem
I sought shelter on the cosy swing.
To and fro, back and forth
it swayed rhythmically
leaving me secure with my thoughts.
An involuntary song I hummed
'Life like a swing goes back and forth
up and down, up and down
keeping the equilibrium intact

makes the experience smooth and joyous
Like the waves that splash
experiences splatter bits of cheer and sorrow
blend these with a smile
life is a journey through thick and thin. '
I rushed in and jotted the words
recollecting the rhythm and pattern.
My heart thumped, and lo behold
the writer in me knocked at the door.
Was it a relief from ennui, or was it a creative spark
that sprinkled little joys along the path?
Was my joy as fulfilling as the relief of the ancient mariner
when the albatross slid from his neck
and fell into the sea?
The ecstasy of writing is unfathomable
There may be a hiatus, but
never the writer shall vanish.

12. THE BLANK PAPER

The fluttering paper, white and bright
alone on the study table
waiting for someone
to redeem it from throes of barrenness
Knowing what gives it fulfilment
it awaits a pen that gives it a life.
So aimless, so distraught,
the blankness seems to bite into its vitals
It dreams of beautiful words
that could change its fate,
the pen that would usher in a new life.
What mysteries, thrills and joys
it could bring in to others' lives
when the white background changes
to blue and the flow of words
touches the hearts of millions.
True that a pen enthrals curious minds
sometimes kindling the dormant hopes
other times tapping the latent emotions.
Imbuing it with a vibrance inimitable
changes its interface.
Enriching its beauty pen lends life
to a blank paper.
Each blank paper, when filled with words

gets a unique identity and wields the power
to translate
dreams into reality
inaction into action
monotony into exhilaration,
shatter myths.
A blank paper's ambitious voyage
into the soul of humanity
is its fulfilment.
And in its blankness is hidden, the unwritten word
that ushers in an era of change.

13. SILENCE

The 'SILENCE PLEASE' poster
swayed to and fro.
The gentle clinking metallic sound
negated the "QUIET ZONE" sign.
A gentle reminder to the library-goers
to maintain a quiet atmosphere
seemed to defeat itself.
"The Peaceful Places" tag went for a toss.
Is silence a lack of sound
or a state of mind?
Is it the unresponsive disposition of the mind
to noise around?
Or a renunciation of the self to surroundings?
Is silence a physical phenomenon
or a spiritual voyage in tranquillity?
Is silence more expressive than words,
or is it an escape from
the inability to express one's feelings?
Speech is silver; silence is gold....
Does it hold good always?
Is it relevant at all times?
As the time passes, change is inevitable.
Silence, once a virtue
could become self-deception.

What was considered 'Golden.'
could be the unvoiced truths of society.
Silence is an enigma
Silence is impalpable
it meanders through life
silencing us sometimes
making us vocal at other times.
Could silence be the golden voice of the era?

14. THE STAGE

The curtains rose, giving a glimpse of the setting.
A street inhabited by the poor
half-broken thatched roofs,
huts embedded into one another
gasping for breath; dingy lane
people clad in tattered clothes.
The stage, a replica of the era
of the British Raj
evoked pathos, anger and distress.
The audience, speechless, lauded the thought.
There was a dried pond
turned into the garbage bin.
Flies and rodents vying for supremacy
buzzed and rattled, scattering the garbage
The odour hit the audience…
The audience wowed at the effects
poverty depicted.
As though it was not enough
Children of the street
fought for the bits of food
scattered on the poorly lit street.
Ah! A sigh escaped from the audience
"So well portrayed!
The British Raj has come alive on the stage.

What a pity. We have not evolved much from that era.
Isn't it true of the present, too?
Why blame the Britishers?
We are no better ......"
The theatre was rife with conflicting thoughts.
A clash of ideas, ideals, values,
divergent views, paradoxical conclusions
The audience went berserk
slippers flew in the air, and landed on the stage
the players sought the refuge of the backscreen.
The curtain came down hurriedly.
Rages flared.
Theatre ransacked; the show abandoned
the deserted auditorium, shut itself from public wrath.
The stage, bereft of any emotions,
stood unaffected.
The show must go on
Tomorrow is yet another day
depicting the characters,
stage set up, backdrop
mike, audio, dialogues
nothing changes for the stage or the theatre.
The GLOBE THEATRE of the Shakespearean era
And the theatre of Delphi of the Greeks?
The stage, a reflection of human emotions,
dreams, aspirations, ambitions
and the eternal conflict between vice and virtue.
Theatre manifests the endless human strife.

15. DIVERSITY

Diversity- a palpable phenomenon
gives a distinctive perspective
to understand the nature of things.
Different perceptions
variety of thoughts
distinct cultures, ethnicity
coming together to make a coherent, liveable society.
Heterogeneity wrapped in
multitudinous colours, shapes and sizes
woven into a fabric reflecting coherence
imbues nature with a unique strength
to combat and resolve the challenges of a diverse universe.
Dissimilarities pave the way for a cohesive society
keeping identity unscathed,
continuing to have their own unique charm and originality.
Diversity- a natural and spiritual marvel,
imbued with a dash of culture and a pinch of races
tangible elements that blend and fuse
to create a universe that vibrates with dissimilarities.
Absorbing, accepting, adjusting, reconciling
the universe venerates the uniqueness of life.

16. JOURNEY

When you begin your journey
hope, aspirations and ambition tag along with you.
A Hope to reach your destination
A strong desire to achieve
A dream to fulfil.
Let not the long winding road,
pitch black and uneven
be a deterrent
let it be the driving force
to propel you to move ahead.
Let your unflinching faith in self
foster your dream
Journey, tedious or stimulating
destination, obscure or attainable
paths rugged or even
Keeping pace with the moving time
takes you nearer to the luring destination.
Chase the time, challenge yourself
Clip, not the wings
Spread them
Zoom past all the barriers
let not the impediments intimidate you
life awaits you with open arms.

17. FOLK ART

Art that delves deep into our cultural roots
artistic creativity fused with local flair
depicting the cultural ethos of a community
handcrafted articles reflecting the local tastes,
motifs reflecting the community values
preserving customs and heritage
Folk Art symbolises the craft of the ancestors
handed over through generations.
The pure magic creates an aura of the bygone times
the fragrance of the soil comes alive
with each article as it takes shape.
The intrinsic patterns woven into the handcrafted articles
neither ostentatious nor flashy,
voice the fading folk art;
yet the struggles of the artisans
to keep the flame of their culture aglow
go unnoticed.
Wading through the high tides of change
the timeless folk art
restoring its lost glory
blending aesthetic beauty with style and nativity
Folk art defies the invasion of technology.

18. EARTH DAY

The ecosystem
its interaction with
living species, natural resources,
basis of earth's existence.
Dynamic in nature, the resilient ecosystem
forms, grows, decays
And from the decayed matter
it rises like a phoenix,
bounces back to its original form.
Earth's
The periodic disturbances
Natural calamities, man-made setbacks
Challenge the resistance of the earth.
Soil, water, air, vegetation
battle with the disruptive forces
to continue their existence.
Earth's abundance
sustains life
its stability and resistance
nurture generations
And yet
It suffers.
Founder of life
strives to sustain itself

Earth Day?
Absurd attempt to revive Earth's glory
last few hours
then begins the game
of plunder and ravage.
Let earth
breath its freshness
absorb its beauty
rejuvenate its decaying resources
then the EARTH shall
Celebrate its 'DAY'.

19. FREEDOM – AN ENIGMA

Freedom- profound, insightful,
inspiring, yet a misguiding word.
'Man is born free but is everywhere in chains.'
Rousseau's perception relevant through the ages,
speaks volumes of human predicament and struggle.
'…. One too like thee: tameless, and swift, and proud.'
Shelley's earnest plea to the West Wind
to endow him with a free spirit
that is tyrannically powerful
that collides through the barricades and spreads its wings.
Does freedom let one break shackles,
let loose the bridle and gallop?
Freedom is mysterious.
The quest for freedom continues….
What, then, is freedom?
Liberty to live on one's terms
or uncurbed freedom bordering on licentiousness?
Is it revolting against the set norms
and living a disorderly life?
Is freedom a lack of scruples and values
or is it a way of life?
A disregard for societal etiquette?

Does freedom give unrestrained liberty to thwart societal norms?
Why this schism?
Remember Tagore's 'Where the mind is without fear'?
Freedom to go beyond the barriers of parochialism
break the boundaries that create walls
live harmoniously, breathe free air bond,
shattering myths of colour and gender.
Freedom, then, is a spiritual journey
through the challenges of limitations.

20. CHAOS

Is beauty hidden in chaos?
Order in disarray?
Human existence ridden with perplexing emotions
drives life through phases of turbulence and tranquillity,
isn't that beauty peeping through the dark clouds?
Tumultuous, complex, intricate relationships,
disorderly society, anarchy at every juncture
Life accepts disruption with a smile
and moves on to embrace that which is elusive.
Order through mayhem, peace through violence
Isn't that a mystery?
Harmony debilitated, hope shattered
conflicts unresolved, chaos rules the universe.
Chaos was not just in the Garden of Eden
when Adam tasted the forbidden fruit
all hell broke loose.
Unimaginable bedlam followed
the wrath of God, flung them headlong into the void
Through chaos was born life away from Heaven.
Old order disobeyed; new order created.

21. DILEMMA

'To be or not to be,'
Hamlet's inner conflict
deeper than the physical pain
reflects his indecisiveness-
should life be lived in utter agony
should it be a compromise
surrendering to the whims of time and society?
Crushing the zeal to live
burden of guilt deepens agony.
Conflicting emotions, like waves,
lashing against the shores of life
enervate the zest for life.
Inner turmoil, external strife
rummage the strings of life
disrupting the equilibrium.
Imprisoned from within
yearning to free self
yet not knowing the path,
will the mind find the panacea for the ills of the mind?
Unaligned, asymmetric thoughts crippling reason
the mind wanders beyond the rational realms.
Irresolute, the soul wades through the troubled waters
to find solace and harmony within the self.
Serenity, the soul of perception

shall gently unravel the mysteries of the conflict
leading to those realms where
dilemma finds its resolve.

• 33 •

22. IDENTITY

'Madam,' he said
'Yes?' the office clerk raised her eyebrow
As though enquiring.
'My ID card is misplaced; could I get another one?
A duplicate one, I mean.'
'Oh, your Identity is misplaced, lost?
And you think I can get it back to you,
I mean, your identity....'
Was she taking a jibe at me?
I could feel the pun.
Involuntarily, I shrugged.
'Madam, whatever you think is right,
kindly do that. I need my identity card at the earliest.'
She clenched her fists in anger
and admonished me.
'You have misplaced yourself and ordering me around?
Get a requisition from your parents.
It will cost....'
She snapped at me.
I squirmed.
It's just an ID card, and she makes me feel
like I have lost myself in the crowd.
Big deal, Id or no, I remain myself
Don't I?

I reassured myself.
Am I not proof enough of my presence?
Is the ID evidence of my existence?
My head reeled.
'Digiyatra' says my face is my ID,
my mobile phone recognises me with my fingerprint,
and the Aadhar Card gives me a unique identity!
The number, then, is my identity.
Who am I?
What am I?
Is my identity limited to a number?
Elsewhere, I read that the face is the index to one's mind.
Oh, the clerk's jibe made sense now.
I have lost myself in the deluge of
multiple identities; which is the true me?
My character, values, and knowledge
each need recognition and an identity.
I cannot draw boundaries around me
to limit myself from ranging beyond the borders.
I am my own identity, with or without the ID card.

23. CREATIVITY

Monotony, boredom
run of the mill, nothing fancy,
aren't these a bane on the mind
that seeks freshness, newness?
A heart that searches for pastures anew,
a mind that explores avenues hitherto unknown,
a soul that yearns for originality,
find enigmatic charm in the challenges of the universe.
Plato's contention of imagination 'twice removed from reality'
defiles the creative urge of the universe.
Life isn't about perfection,
it is all about juxtaposing the binaries
that urge the human mind to go beyond the limitations
and grasp that which is elusive and unfamiliar.
Isn't life progressive in its nature?
Stagnation extinguishes the spark,
while growth ignites innovativeness.
Life rejuvenates through newness.
It propagates itself in innovative forms.
Isn't an idea itself a creative thought?
Art is a creative expression of the mind,
science is innovative thoughts,
technology is scientific creativity.
Creativity is values redefined,

innovation is distinctive knowledge,
that which defies the monotony of life is creativity.

24. EQUALITY

"All animals are equal, but some are more equal than others."
George Orwell proclaims in his "Animal Farm"
Equality is a namesake; it favours the elite,
and the larger section gets just a glimpse of equality.
What is equality?
Is it social justice, a legal right or an ethical concept?
Where the societal layers differentiate
the masses from the sophisticated,
the middle order elevates itself above the lower classes,
the upper strata degrades the middle class,
religion separates human beings,
caste and creed draw boundaries,
language demarcates states,
what equality are we witnessing?
Equality is mysterious; it swirls around us
fascinates us, prances around us,
but is never in our grip.
Yet we crave for equality
seeking it in all our tasks
looking for it in the housework and office space.
Fighting, exploiting, surrendering
We struggle for equal rights
equal opportunities.
Gender equality, workplace equality,

equality in the eyes of the law,
unbiased approach to colour and creed….
isn't that far-fetched?
A dream that vanishes faster than lightning,
an illusion that bursts like a bubble in a moment.
Abilities and skills vary; where is equality?
Opportunities, respect and mutual understanding
are the soul of equality.
Is equality situational, contextual
that flashes like a glow-worm
sounds lyrical
but has neither power nor value
in the larger purview of life,
confines itself to the privileged
eludes the deprived.
Equality is a misnomer.
It has found a place in constitutional rights
but has never placed itself in the context of reality.
Equality is a remote value,
a mirage that is but is not.

25. HARMONY

Balanced emotions, steady relationships,
a blend of symmetry and proportion
harmony is somewhat akin to mathematics.
a slight variation, a minor departure
causes imbalance.
Harmony, the soul of the universe
establishes, nurtures and
perpetuates human relations,
enriches the bond with nature.
Vital to existence, harmony
the harbinger of peace and unity,
accords with the natural and human world
to bring in equilibrium.
Earth's rhythmic movements
in harmony with the scheme of things
is the truth of our existence.
The tilt on its axis is in tune with the
rotation and revolution
isn't that a harmonious relationship between the earth
and its living things?
Isn't the position of the planets and the sun
in accordance with the nature of things?
Harmony is the philosophy of the universe
where the heart, mind and soul align

to usher in peaceful co-existence.

• 41 •

26. PERSPECTIVE

'No marks, please, no marks…'
The girl in the advertisement, hands folded
implores the unseen God.
And then, the ad shows a cream
'NO MARKS'
and the jingle
'From marks to no marks…'
astonished at the change in the word impact
stunned at the innovative thought
amazed at the new approach
I delved deep into the face cream ad.
What an insightful, creative idea!
A strong 'NO' with a more robust 'YES.'
a face cream that keeps the skin glowing
and, of course, no scars!
Isn't that a new outlook on 'MARKS'?
Marks that measure knowledge, skill and ability
just changed into a beauty cream advertisement!
What a perspective!
A dot in the centre of a whiteboard
let not be the focal point.
Why not the white and the board, too?
How incredibly profound!
Arjuna's 'eye of the fish' has a new perspective now.

Attitude matters.
To tread on 'The road not taken'
is challenging yet rewarding.
As the spirit of life
scales new heights,
wanders into the horizon,
swims against the tide
a new approach to life awaits us.

27. BREATH

The azure blue curtains
swayed to the rhythmic breeze
the tinkling melodies of the metal chime
set an aura of tranquillity
the soft footfall of the attenders
the gentle closing of the swinging doors....
just the right ambience
so serene, so soothing.

The machine beeping
vitals fluctuating
agitated nurse
anxious relatives

The gasps and the heavy breathing
the restless body shuddering
the agony of approaching 'end.'
each breath is so precious, so dear
never did we value breath so much as now
Breathing is so natural, so effortless!
As the breath is parting ways
The urge to hold on to yet another breath

to grab life from the cruel hands of death
to feel the air through the nostrils
to revel in the last few breaths
ah! Isn't life all about breathing?
Life is breath,
breath, the essence of life.

The oxygen cylinder detached
the pipes removed
the sheet over the face
and
it has ended.
No more breathing
No more sighs
No more gasps.
Breath, the betrayer.

28. LIBRARY

I am a living being
I emote, I feel, I think
I live through the years.
Living the life of many
authors, editors, readers, critics
each one's perspective, each one's thoughts
come alive where I reside.
Tons of books, from comics to magazines
Newspapers to journals
I am limitless.
As I watch them bury their heads deep into books
a smile lights up my face.
Their enjoyment is beyond the four walls of the library
It transcends the physical realms,
transports them to a world away from
strife and struggles, woes and sufferings.
The mischievous smile of the corner table reader
the disbelief in the eyes of the side table reader
the serenity of that middle-aged uncle
the secret admiration in that young boy's eyes
and the yearning in that young lass' countenance
infinite emotions, endless love
I am ecstatic.
Their joy is my fulfilment,

their purpose is my ambition,
and their happiness is my intent.
What more would I wish for?
Surrounded by stories, poems, ideas, thoughts
spirituality, philosophy, facts and fiction
reality and imagination....
I am a galore of hues
splashing vibrant colours across lives
driving away monotony,
ushering in a zest for life
and igniting the spark to soar.
Who says libraries are a thing of the past?
I will neither be outdated nor obsolete
as long as writers write and readers read.

29. THE ALBUM

Gathering the moments
holding on to the memories
some faded, some dim
background waning, turning mild yellow
faces unknowable,
yet the photo album
still resonates with memories.
When was the photo taken?
Which studio did we go to?
What was the occasion?
History, geography and economics
(yes, not physics and chemistry)
deeply embedded in a photo.
A vital role of logistics
studio, location, fame, and I
not to forget affordability.
Pros and cons weighed painstakingly,
loaded with excitement,
looked forward to the photo session.
Remember, there was only one family photo,
so you better be cheerful and ready.
Hours of preparation
deciding on clothes, hairstyle, and
who is where in the photo!

That done (a major accomplishment)
Should the studio come home,
or does the house visit the photographer?
A dilemma that was not so easy to resolve.
The elders consulted; the youngsters pacified
studio coming home vetoed
visiting the studio voted.
The never-ending 'smile, please.'
'Tilt your neck, bend your head'
'Push that lock of hair behind the ear....'
Ah! Those moments of utter chaos
bring a smile as memories flood.
A photo, an event, or a celebration
no wonder the album is a cherished possession

30. BRIDGES

A doorway to connect
a pathway to bind
a link to join
and a harness to cohere
BRIDGES bridge the gap.
How strange a metal framework
builds relationships!
Boulders bridge the gap!
Ram Setu to Lakshman Jhula
Howrah Bridge to The Sea Link
Atal Setu to Pamban Bridge
what are these bridges?
Physical entities that connect,
whether boulders or iron
wooden or ropes,
bridges bring in the joy of togetherness.
Bridges a foundation for human relationships and growth.
Whether for a cosmic or commercial purpose
bridges are doorways to changing perspectives.
Bridging the gap between communities
aligning feelings with thought
narrowing down the void
bringing down the differences
erasing the parochial views

***BRIDGES** usher in an era of unity and progress.*

• 51 •

Acknowledgements

Everyone who has been an integral part of my journey as a poet, SHEROES—Sairee Chahal madam, Shiny Hoque, Shruthi Chatterjee, Aaradhna Agarwal, Achla Nagar, Girija Menon, and all the readers on SHEROESwho have read, liked, and appreciated my poems, given input and feedback.

I would like to acknowledge the following poets and authors of yesteryear whose lines and titles I have quoted. These poets have greatly impacted my poems, and I draw inspiration from their poems and ideas.

Robert Frost, P.B. Shelley, George Orwell, Rabindranath Tagore, Louisa May Alcott, Shakespeare and Rousseau.

Author Bio

Shashikala Gadepally has embarked on a journey with her newfound passion for writing. Her creative urge and imaginative faculty have given her wings to explore the unknown realms.

She has authored several books in various genres, including fiction and poetry, with themes ranging from socio-political suspense thrillers to romance and human relationships.

Her favourite authors are P.G. Wodehouse and James Hadley Chase.

Her simple, lucid language enhances readability, and the easy flow of words connects the reader to the storyline.

Her eBooks published on Amazon Kindle are collections of poems on the relationship between nature and human beings, human relationships and the conflict between nature and man.

Her debut novel, The Absent Citizen, focuses on a civilised society in which social and ethical values have been neglected.

Her collections of short stories are Beyond the Horizon, Till Eternity…., The Untold Sagas, A Twist in the Tale, Living in Shadows and The Dark Realms.

Her collections of poems are Verses of Life, Silent Musings, Waves and Petals, Symphonies - ruminations of Fragments and 'An Ode to Love'.

She started her author journey at sixty, and there is no looking back.

www.ingramcontent.com/pod-product-compliance
Lightning Source LLC
Chambersburg PA
CBHW021810150726
47989CB00004B/1869